DON'T JUST COACH!

UNLOCKING YOUR TEAM'S POTENTIAL

BEN MORTON

Foreword by David Clutterbuck

VAEO

Enter the immersive world of VAEO

VAEO, from mPowr Publishing, is a series of captivating ecosystems that you access and explore by engaging many different senses. Layering sound, imagery, text, virtual interaction, and other sensory experiences, VAEO brings the author's world into your environment. With your printed book, a smartphone or tablet, and your headphones, you can broaden the scope of each page in your home, office, or wherever you happen to be. As you read this VAEO, scan the QR codes found throughout to access gateways into the virtual realms and discover a whole new dimension to your journey.

How to get the most from your VAEO title...

Step One: Download a QR code reader onto your smartphone or tablet. We recommend *i-nigma*, which works well with the colour codes.

Step Two: Scan the QR code below. Follow the instructions to register your *Don't Just Manage—Coach!* VAEO.

Step Three: Scan the gateway codes in the book to access audio and other virtual content. You can listen by using headphones, the built-in speakers, or external speakers.

Step Four: Follow the simple instructions on screen to experience the virtual content.

To Jo and Freya

my amazing wife and wonderful daughter

Acknowledgements

Coaching and leadership are about people and people made this book.

I am hugely grateful to those individuals who gave up their time to talk to me about their experiences of coaching and developing their people. I believe that the book is so much richer for the inclusion of their real life experiences as manager coaches. The case studies are all anonymous and as such the names of these great leaders are not included. You all know who you are and I am extremely grateful for your support—thank you.

This book started as a few PowerPoint slides following a spark of inspiration. The finished product is very different and that is a result of two great people fanning the initial spark of an idea.

Firstly, I must thank Richard Nugent for his continual support, guidance, encouragement and coaching. Without him I wouldn't be where I am now and for that I am hugely grateful. I consider it a privilege to call him a colleague and a friend. Thank you.

Secondly, thanks go to Stephanie Walters, another brilliant coach in her own right. She read the initial version of my book when it was a forty-slide e-book written in PowerPoint. Her gentle yet direct feedback was the catalyst for turning this book into what it became.

My personal journey as a coach has been accelerated greatly thanks to time spent working with Dave Reynolds, my coaching supervisor. By skilfully pushing me to reflect more, and on a deeper level, my skills as a coach have increased dramatically over time. Reflecting on your coaching performance alone can be difficult—Dave helped me to see the wood amongst the trees.

Finally, there are not enough words to thank my amazing wife, Jo. Without knowing it, you have made it possible for me to write this book. You have done this by standing by me, encouraging me and doing all you can to support me whilst starting my business. Whenever I had a wobble you were there to give me a reassuring reality check. You have done all of this whilst leading your own amazing career and looking after our wonderful daughter Freya.

Writing this book and starting my business has been hard work—and great fun. Jo, you have made it all possible.

Thank you.

Foreword

by David Clutterbuck

A few years ago, I gathered the stories of dozens of employees in different organisations about their experience of going on a "line manager as coach course", or when their own manager had been on a similar course. Their stories were depressingly similar, overall. The initial enthusiasm of the course quickly wore off as the reality of coaching in the real world asserted itself. Their direct reports didn't want to be coached, and it wasn't long before a crisis or two impelled the manager back into directive behaviours. Mostly, the direct reports (and the manager) breathed a sigh of relief. When coaching is done in an amateur way, it is clumsy and uncomfortable. And when it is done competently, it is still uncomfortable for the coachee, because it requires them to think and to take greater personal accountability for their own performance and development.

The line manager and his or her team comprise a system and systems theory tells us that changing one part of the system leads the rest to pull it back to how it was before. This was what had happened to these managers. Researchers, such as Stephen Ferrar, have identified a lengthy list of reasons why line-manager coaching fails—among them the difficulty of being totally honest in a boss-subordinate relationship and the tendency for hierarchy to push people into parent-child behaviours.

So does that mean that line managers should give up on the idea of being coaches to their teams? Far from it.

Experiments in a variety of organisations, both commercial and educational, suggest that the key is to develop a coaching culture—an environment, where coaching and mentoring are part of the normal tasks and behaviours of the team. Some of the lessons we learned from these experiments include that, to change the team system, it is important that:

- Everyone in the team learns about coaching together (at the same time, over a sufficient period to achieve a change in mindset—this is not about acquiring a skill, it's about developing a collective way of thinking).
- Everyone takes responsibility for both their own learning and everyone else's.
- There is a collective team-development plan.
- The leader supports the team in taking a coaching approach to current and real issues that affect team performance.

With a supportive team behind him or her, the line manager has a much stronger chance of sustaining the momentum of coaching. Equally important, however are two other factors: the support they receive from outside the team and the line manager's own, genuine desire to be a coach (and to be coached).

Support from outside the team comes from a variety of sources. Having a database of further learning materials is helpful, especially if they are online. Opportunities to compare notes and co-coach with peers are also effective in maintaining and improving a coaching mindset. Additionally, professional supervision, which is increasingly common in a number of countries, including the UK, can give the coach deeper insight and greater confidence in their ability to support change in other people.

The line manager's internal motivation to learn and to help others to learn seems to be a defining criterion for success as a coach. Among practical things the line-manager coach can do to continue to grow in the role are to be coached (and learn from how their own coach works) and to read widely in and around the topics of coaching and mentoring.

Continuous development in the coaching role is essential, both to prevent regression to pre-coaching behaviours and mindsets, but also because the initial skills and approaches taught in coaching courses rapidly become inadequate, when exposed to the reality of day-to-day coaching. Time and again, coaches tell me how liberating it is to learn that they don't have to follow the GROW model—that they have long felt the need to outgrow it. Instead, they gradually accumulate the confidence and the knowledge to relegate GROW to just one of the tools (and often one of the least useful) they can employ in helping a colleague with the quality of their thinking. Like professional external coaches, internal coaches have the opportunity and potential to move through various stages of coach maturity. Doing so has major positive implications for their later career success, because coaching is a critical skill and behaviour that we need from tomorrow's leaders.

Don't Just Manage—Coach! positions coaching, and becoming a better coach in the workplace, firmly in the context of continuous self-improvement. It provides insights into what prevents line managers being good coaches and practical advice on how to overcome these obstacles. It makes sure that coaches, who are at the very beginning of their experience, are comfortable with GROW, but then offers guidance and challenge into how to move beyond the relatively simplistic basics and develop their own coaching style. (It's like first learning to ride a bicycle with stabilisers, then abandoning them, when you have confidence and instinctive balance.) Whether you are a beginner as a line-manager coach, or one who is looking to enhance their skills, you will at the very least find some useful hints and tips in these pages.

David Clutterbuck is regarded as a leading global authority on coaching and mentoring. Author of more than fifty books, he brings a wealth of practical experience and leading edge research to developing leaders at the top. A successful entrepreneur in his own right, David makes serious management topics accessible through humour, story and provoking perspectives.

Contents

Introduction   12

1 - Coaching and Leadership   15

2 - The Manager-Coach Trap   25

3 - It Starts with Me   31

4- Be Aware of Your Head Tapes   39

5 - Fair-Weather Coaching   43

6 - Get Clear on the Goals   49

7 - Focus on Performance   55

8 - Challenge   61

9 - Coaching is for Everyone   65

10 - Reaching Elite Performance   71

11 - Be Specific   75

12 - It Goes Both Ways   79

13 - Be of Service   85

14 - Be Proactive, Be Flexible   93

15 - The GROW Model   103

16 - Beyond GROW   111

Appendix   122

Introduction

In some ways it is easier to begin by describing what this book is not. *Don't Just Manage—Coach!* is not designed to be a comprehensive how-to guide for coaching. There are so many great books available covering that topic so my intention is not to write another. Nor is this a book designed for those who are totally new to coaching with no prior experience at all.

So what is it and who is it for?

Coaching is becoming more and more prevalent within organisations today. Whilst some organisations employ external coaches, many are training their own. This is a book for all of the internal coaches out there who are quietly going about their work. It is for those managers who believe in the value of investing time in developing their people to achieve great things. It is for the team leaders who want to create highly efficient, high performing teams. This is a book for anybody who wants to make coaching—

"The way we do things round here."

In my experience of training coaches and coaching coaches, I have noticed that there are a number of mistakes that manager-coaches often unwittingly make. What's more, I have made most, if not all, of these mistakes myself during my own coaching journey. I've also come to realise that there are some common misconceptions that still exist about what coaching is and what coaching is not.

This book is therefore written with the aim of shining a light on those common mistakes, dispelling the myths and giving you the tools and insights to avoid them. It's a book designed to help accelerate your development as a coach by learning from the mistakes of others.

My hope is that this book will enable you to become the leader you are capable of becoming. By adopting a coaching style you'll find that your people are more engaged and more willing to work for you with blood, sweat and tears. What's more, by coaching your people you'll be able to unlock the full potential of your team.

In many ways this book is my attempt to bring to life one of my favourite Chinese proverbs:

"The wise man learns from his mistakes, the wiser man learns from the mistakes of others."

Download Pack

Chapter One

Coaching & Leadership
Two Sides of the Same Coin

"Great leaders understand that **every** team member is **unique** and **every** team member adds **value. "**

I believe that there is a clear, close and incredibly significant link between coaching and leadership. To be a great leader you need to understand how to get the very best levels of performance from your people. To get the very best from your people, you need to know how best to support them, how to coach them.

I also believe that leadership and coaching has never been more important to the success of teams and organisations than it is right now. The leadership capability of any team or organisation directly shapes its culture, how innovative its products and services are and the experience its customers have. This direct line between the ability of the organisation's management community to lead, inspire and develop their people is why coaching is now so crucial.

Year on year we see more and more surveys that report the most common reasons people choose to leave an organisation. One of the most common reasons that consistently appears in the findings is that people leave due to poor management, leadership or a lack of development. How many times have you read or heard this quote?

"People don't leave bad organizations, they leave bad **managers.""**

If there was ever a **compelling reason** to invest time, energy and resources into developing our **ability** to support our people then surely this is it. For me, the most effective way for any company to **reduce** its **recruitment costs** is to invest money in developing the **leadership capability** of its managers. It's a **simple** formula. Better management equals lower staff turnover, equals lower recruitment costs. If you consider the average cost to hire a new starter in

2013

was around

$1500

for staff and

£4000

for managers, you would at worst **break even** on your **investment**. At best, you would **significantly increase** performance, improve results and positively impact the bottom line. For anybody trying to **build** a business case for some form of **training investment** then surely this must be it.

That may be a compelling business case for the organisation but I often hear managers ask what's in it for them. The answer is a very similar formula to that I described above. Better management equals lower staff turnover, equals less time recruiting and getting new recruits up to speed. It also equals more engaged staff who are willing and able to successfully take on more challenging projects. Ultimately, for you as a manager, the outcome is leading a team that's a pleasure to lead because your people are motivated and successful.

Coaching is happening more and more in organisations today and recent research from the Chartered Institute of Personnel and Development shows that:

Coaching is consistently ranked within the
most effective leadership
and talent-development solutions.

45%

of organisations plan to utilise coaching to drive
organisational performance in the next two years.

53%

of Private Sector organisations believe their
leaders lack the skills to effectively coach their people.

So, for you as a manager this is really saying that coaching your people is one of the most effective things you can do to develop your people. It's also saying that if your organisations isn't already using coaching to improve the business then the chances are that they soon will. Finally, it's telling you that there are lots of managers and leaders out there who don't yet have the skills to effectively coach their people. So this is your opportunity to be one of the minority that does.

With this background in mind, I think that it's useful to begin by exploring, just briefly, a few definitions of exactly what we mean when we talk about management, leadership and coaching.

The word *management* has Latin roots originating from the word *manus*, meaning *by hand*. It is therefore about managing productivity, tasks or resources. For me, management is more about telling and doing and less about showing and inspiring.

On the other hand, *leadership* has Anglo-Saxon or Norse roots, deriving from the words *path* or *journey*. It's about looking forwards; it's about creating a vision of where you are heading and how things will be in the future. The best leaders have the ability to align people to that vision whilst motivating them to work passionately and relentlessly towards its fulfilment.

Coaching is about helping your employees become more effective, it's about improving their performance and it's about solutions. In this respect coaching is also about the future and a development journey that you can take with your team. At its most fundamental level, coaching is about supporting and involving them in the process and investing your time in their development.

Having looked at the definitions we can start to see some similarities and parallels between leadership and coaching. Both are about the future, they are solutions focused, about making things better and moving forwards.

In adopting a management style that embraces coaching, you are becoming a leader. In other words you are helping your people to see their future, to realise their potential and to be inspired by what is possible.

In becoming a manager-coach you are challenging and developing your employees' skills and abilities to achieve the best possible performance results, and to function as self-sufficiently as possible. Yes, it initially feels like more work for you, but you will quickly reap the rewards of the investment you have made in your team. And it *is* an investment—never a cost. They will reward you with hard work, commitment and productivity—what we commonly hear referred to as engagement.

TheCoachingandLeadershipStory

Organization: **Major British Retailer**
Coach: **Store Manager**
Team Member: **All staff in his store**

Interviewing Steven filled me with confidence about management capability in the UK. The press and industry media can often present less than positive reports about the current status of our management capability and Steven's story is the antidote to that. Having finished interviewing Steven I genuinely felt confident, humbled and inspired. This is Steven's story.

Steven manages a large format retail store working for one of the UK's biggest retailers.

He began by telling me about an individual in his team who was not performing well in their role. The individual was his stock control manager; it was a demanding job that was heavily based around process and routine. Despite struggling with the role he had an incredible work ethic and was a very humble man. Steven said that in his early days as a manager he would have rushed in and tackled the poor performance.

> Seven years ago I would have said that you're not doing a good job, you're taking your paycheque so you need to crack on and sort it out.

But that is not what he did on this occasion. Over a period of four weeks he observed the team member and focused on building a sense of rapport with him. This was by just giving him time—five minutes here and ten minutes there. Steven calls this approach Stop-Coach-Go and described the impact that it had on this occasion:

22

By using Stop-Coach-Go I was able to get to know him and I found out that he had not been living in the UK for long. He was struggling to adjust to living here as well as struggling with the job. His family and daughter had not yet moved to the country and that was making things even harder for him. I tried to put myself in his shoes and think about how well I would perform in his situation. I absolutely wouldn't and I don't think many people would.

I took him for lunch so that I could understand his situation and we could work out a way forward. Now that's not something I had time for, in a £1.8 million store you just don't have time for that but it was really important for me to understand what sort of person he was—to give him another opportunity.

So we gave him another opportunity working on the counters. Because of the connection with me, because I took the time out, he was really loyal to me. He really wanted to listen and work with me to understand how we were going to get this tough department performing and how we were going to get them behind him. Being a stock control manager, his role was previously all process whereas counters is about people. It was only through getting to know him that I realised that the person inside wasn't a process person. He was naturally engaging and that is what counters are all about.

I told him that we were on a journey and that I would be with him every step of the way on that journey.

The most powerful thing about Steven's story for me is his approach to leadership. His belief in his people and carving out the time to support them has led to amazing results. Whilst Steven has never been trained as a coach he understands that his role as a manager is to help his team members be more effective and help them to improve their performance. Whilst doing this he was talking about the future, talking about solutions and describing the journey. That is what being a manager-coach is about and in doing so, Steven has become an exceptional leader.

The end of Steven's story is equally as inspiring. Here's how he described it to me:

Eventually his wife and daughter moved and settled in our country and they have since had another baby. To watch him gain in confidence from the little successes that we celebrated and shared with the team was amazing.

He now runs one of the best counters in the UK and to see him walking around with Directors because they want to understand and replicate his success is fantastic.

The highlight for me was seeing him when six senior Directors came to visit the counters. He said to me, 'Boss, will you be there?' I said no. This is your time and it's your success—I'll meet them at the door and then it's over to you. I visited the counters in the morning before the visit and the atmosphere was electric.

After that visit we chatted and I said to him that this wasn't the end of his journey. It was the start of another journey.

Chapter Two

The Manager-Coach Trap

"Management is doing things right, **leadership** is doing the **right things."**

Peter Drucker

believe the manager-coach trap is the single biggest challenge for manager-coaches and it is a mistake that so many people unwittingly make. The problem lies in the journey that the vast majority of managers have taken to reach their current position. For most of us, the journey involves being promoted from a functional expert, somebody doing the doing, to a manager who now has responsibility for looking after a team of doers. This journey to leadership and management is by no means wrong; it's merely the natural way that most careers unfold and how the majority of organizations fill their management positions. Whilst it's not wrong, it does present a challenge.

If we break down the role of any manager, we can see that there are generally three components to the job:

Doing things

This is typically what attracted you to your profession or career in the first place. If you're in finance it will be running the numbers, if you're in sales it will be selling, if you're in marketing it will be creating campaigns and so on.

Managing things

This involves managing things such as projects, budgets, campaigns or any other resources that you are responsible for. They are the sorts of things that we tend to be given very specific and highly measurable targets for. It is most likely that these are the activities that we will be reviewed against in our annual appraisal and are explicitly linked to the organisation's corporate goals or targets in some way.

Leading people

This is about inspiring your people, sharing a positive vision for the future, empowering them to act and supporting their growth. It is the activity that we intuitively know can make a significant difference to organisational performance but can often feel intangible and difficult to measure. Whilst there is a great deal of research available that demonstrates the financial benefits of great leadership, many organisations struggle to measure it themselves.

The fact that leading people is at the bottom of this list is the cause of the manager-coach trap. This is why so many people are failing to be the leaders that they could be, the leaders that they are capable of becoming. Very few people, with perhaps the exception of those joining the Armed Forces and one or two other professions, set out in their career wanting to be a leader. For most people it is a by-product of promotion and this is exactly what creates the danger of the manager-coach trap.

When the pressure is on or when we are stressed, most of us default to a natural prioritisation of our to-do list. This prioritisation normally looks something like this:

Firstly, we revert to doing things, the things that drew us to our chosen career in the first place. We do this for a number of reasons. One reason is that we like to fall back on activities that are within our comfort zone. Stress is often created out of a lack of certainty about the future which neuroscience now shows to be a critical need for the brain (David Rock; Your Brain at Work, 2009). A lack of certainty creates a strong threat response in the brain; activating the same region that lights up during our fight or flight response. Similarly however, rewarding our need for certainty triggers a strong reward response and releases a shot of dopamine, the *happy* hormone. So, in tackling the tasks that lie well within our comfort zone we provide a short-term stress relief triggered by a short burst of dopamine.

On a similar but more basic level, reverting to doing things allows us to focus on the things that brought us to our chosen profession in the first place. This shifts our focus from our problems, to activities that we enjoy and thus changes our state to a much more positive and productive one. The danger here is that our addiction to the chemical high we get from a quick shot of dopamine means that we can become busy fools. We fall into the trap of spending our time in doing the activities we enjoy and those that we can easily accomplish rather than doing the activities that will give us the greatest payoff.

Secondly, we focus on managing things. The reason for this is that we tend to be measured on the things that we have to manage. The old adage of—what gets measured, gets done—really kicks in. Once again, modern neuroscience gives us an insight into what brain activity is driving this behaviour. David Rock also identified that we have a fundamental status need that triggers the exact same response as our certainty need. The thought of failing to deliver upon our objectives generates a threat to our status which we respond to. 'What will my manager think if I fail to deliver on this? If I don't deliver will I be viewed as less effective than my colleagues?'

These are the sorts of voices we often hear in our heads that drive and trigger our responses. Whilst the outcome is the same—working hard to deliver—the motivation varies from individual to individual. Some are driven by a strong away-from response, they will do what ever it takes not to fail or let somebody down. Some on the other hand are motivated by a towards response, 'If I achieve this or over deliver I will be rewarded with a promotion'.

Because most of us didn't set out to become leaders, and most organisations don't measure managers against how they lead their people, the leading-people element of our role goes to the bottom of the to-do list and this is the manager-coach trap. But, the best leaders have learned to flip this natural ordering.

To overcome it we need to get really clear on *why* we are managers and the type of leader we want to be. We then have to force ourselves to step off the hamster wheel and find the time to start thinking, planning and supporting our teams; to be the brilliant leaders, managers and coaches that we are capable of becoming.

So, how do we do it?

Chapter Three

It Starts with Me

"Leadership is the **simplest thing** in the world because it's just plain **you "**

Field Marshall The Viscount Slim

Whilst I absolutely believe that coaching and leadership are not about you as an individual, I do believe that it starts with you.

As leaders, our role is to inspire and motivate those around us. As a coach our role is to quieten our own thinking so that we can give all of our attention to supporting those we are coaching. In either role, leader or coach, we are there to serve those with whom we have the privilege and pleasure to work.

By looking after ourselves (Me) and managing our own state we can look after and support our teams (Us) so that they can get on and do the doing, delivering the objectives (The Results) for the business.

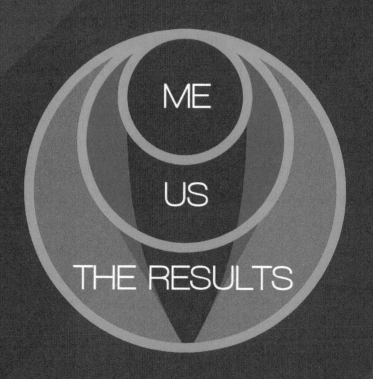

I have introduced this model, or variations of it, in hundreds of training workshops. In every one of these I have asked the participants to think about a typical day or week and estimate the amount of time that they allocate to each of the three elements. The results are always the same. The vast majority of managers spend around 70-80% of their time doing the doing themselves. Sometime this is even as high as 90-95%. At best this leaves 20-30% of their time to invest in themselves or their teams, which I'd suggest is far too little.

The **ideal situation** is to hold the three parts roughly in **balance**, on average. By **managing your time** and allocating it between the **three elements** you are able to hit the sweet spot of **leading and coaching**.

This equal allocation of one third of your time being dedicated to **you**, **your team** and the **results** is of course somewhat unrealistic. There will be times when the demands of a **specific project** mean that you need to place a lot more **focus** on the results yourself—and that is absolutely fine. That is the correct thing to do in **those** circumstances. But, when the work has been delivered or the pressure eases then it is time to **redress the balance**. You may need to focus on **supporting** your team again. You will probably also need to focus on **yourself** and recharging the batteries.

Consider this familiar situation. It's mid-December and you have been under a lot of pressure at work due to a number of **major projects** that you need to **deliver**. You've not had any time off work, other than weekends, since August when you took a one-week holiday in the sun. Your partner wanted you to take two weeks off but you said that you were just **too busy** at work—you really could only take one week. The **cumulative effect** of this pressure and lack of time off is a build up of **cortisol**, the **stress hormone**, in your body.

Cortisol's prime purpose is to **prepare** the human body for **action**—it controls our **fight or flight** response and makes us **super alert**. In order to do this it turns off what it **considers** to be non-vital bodily processes or functions. One of these is our immune system. We are not designed to have large quantities of cortisol pumping through our veins for protracted periods of time. So, the effect of that pressure at work is a continual drip, drip, drip of cortisol into our body suppressing our immune system. Christmas comes and your body shuts down—you suddenly have the flu, a cold or a sore throat. 'Why does this always happen?' you ask yourself. It's because you have not got the balance right.

The first step when getting off the treadmill therefore has to be understanding where you currently invest your time and then looking to redress the balance. In doing this we start to take back some time, take back control thus enabling us to think, lead and coach our people to the best of our ability.

Some things to try:

For each of the last five days, consider how much of your time has been spent on activity that focuses on you, your team and the tasks at hand.

Think about and commit to paper three things that you can *start* doing right now to create more balance.

Think about and commit to paper three things you can *stop* doing right now to shift the balance.

TheItStartsWithMeStory

Organization: **Major British Retailer**

Coach: **Store Manager**

Team Member: **All staff in his store**

This is another story from Steven. Later in the same interview with him I asked how he would describe his management or leadership style. He began by telling me about his *Three Cs*—he likes to be Calm, Confident and Caring. However, Steven very quickly told me that he didn't always have this approach. In fact, he said that in the early part of his career he was working too quickly, making decisions too rapidly and as a result lost a lot of good people. What was the catalyst for this significant change? Here it is in Steven's own words.

I've been on a journey. I've been the manager that didn't have time for his people. If I can put it simply, when I became a Store Manager I was just a manager. I could manage anything through process and routine. What I did was move from one process to the next—almost like a bee.

But then you stop and notice the bodies behind you. At that moment you realise I'm really good at this but I've got nobody with me.

It really hit home when I moved from one store to another and people said to me, 'It's been great working for you Steven, but I wouldn't like to do it again.'

They said that I was a great manager and they'd learnt so much from me about process and routine. But they also said that it had been so hard and that they were really knackered.

That made me sit down and think about what I needed to do differently. I realised that I didn't know the people I was working with. At that point I decided that I wanted to start leading people rather than managing them along with processes and routines.

I now think that management is really easy. But to lead people, you really need to stop and give them time. It could be 10-15 minutes, it could be just going and having a cup of tea with them. I like to use Stop-Coach-Go. This is about just taking the time to listen to and help your team members, I really concentrate on listening to the person I'm with. I like to get really clear on how to achieve results and move forward with what it is that the person wants to do themselves.

What struck me from the first few minutes of my conversation with Steven was that his focus was heavily on his people. When describing his current approach to management, he spoke about the numbers or the performance of his store very little. To those unaccustomed with the retail environment this may not seem that significant, but it is hugely significant. As Steven continued to speak it became evident that he had an absolute belief that in looking after himself, he was able to support his people and that would allow him to deliver the results. And deliver the results it did. Here's what Steven said next:

It's never about the results, the results will happen. So far I've never had bad results in any store that I've worked in. The engagement survey is what's really important and I've never had a bad one of those either.

I recently took one of my new operations managers out for a cup of coffee, we actually had two coffees and chatted for two hours. Now I haven't got two hours in my day, I just don't. But you can choose to think that way or you can find a way to make the time. I was able to help him see things from a different angle and to support him.

I normally start any conversation with them talking about their family, sports that they are interested in or what ever it may be going on for them. You are only able to do that if you take time out to get to know them, not to coach them, just to get to know them. This means that later on when you need people to help deliver something—they want to because they feel part of it, because you have that connection.

This is a compelling example of the impact you can have by looking after yourself so that you can support your team to deliver the results. Steven's story is all the more remarkable for the fact that he works in the high pressured, numbers-driven environment of retail. By slowing down, by focusing on giving time and support to his people he has achieved so much more.

When he looks behind him now, there is a strong team of motivated, happy people who are ready to go the extra mile for him.

Chapter Four

Be Aware of
Your Head Tapes

"Change
your thoughts and
you
change the world."

Norman Vincent Peale

We all have **voices** in our heads that can sow the seeds of doubt, **motivate** us to **act** or cloud our **thinking** and **judgment.** The voices in our heads, or mind-talk, are generally **developed** over a long period of time and are based upon our **values, life experiences, friends** and **family**.

The problem is not so much that our **mind-talk** exists, the problem is that we may not always be **aware** of the **impact** it is having on our **thinking, feelings** and **actions**. Imagine an old music cassette tape that has just one or two songs on it. If you were to **play that tape** on a

40

continual loop, over and over again, those few songs would eventually be stuck in your mind. You'd be singing or humming the tune to yourself all day long.

Our minds work in a similar way. As a result of our mind-talk we tend to run and repeat a series of tapes in our minds that may or may not be helpful . Either way, these tapes become stuck in our minds driving us towards a specific course of action. This then prevents us from seeing other options or fresh insights.

When manager-coaches observe their team members behaving in problematic ways, they can often find it difficult to talk to them about it. This may be because they are nervous about how their team member may react and that the meeting will turn into a difficult conversation.

The key thing for us to remember is that the mental tapes that we run in our heads are based upon how we *think* the meeting may unfold. It's not necessarily how it *will* unfold.

The problem isn't so much that we run these head tapes in the first place, it lies in the fact that we don't rationalise them and take control of our own thought process. We act on our unhelpful head tapes and believe the feelings that they generate.

The first step along the road to being confident in tackling these situations is to learn to be aware of the head tapes that we are running. Once we are aware of this internal chatter that is taking place in our minds, we can begin replacing the unhelpful tapes with more productive ones.

Here's an example. An unhelpful head tape may be something like, 'What if they are upset by the feedback that I share?'

If we are aware of our thinking we could reframe this in a more helpful way, thus replacing the head tape. We might say, 'I'm providing them with feedback to genuinely help them improve their performance so they shouldn't get upset. Even if they do, they won't be upset for ever.'

Some things to try:

Think of a specific time, a person you have to deal with or an awkward conversation you need to have.

What was the head tape that you ran?
Is that head tape useful or unhelpful?
If it is unhelpful how can you reframe it?

Concentrate on and be aware of your own head tapes. The next time that you catch yourself running an unhelpful tape, stop and start playing your more useful, more productive version.

Chapter Five
Fair-Weather Coaching

> **" A ship is safe in harbour, but that's not what ships are for. "**
>
> *William G.T. Shedd*

Fair-weather coaching is in some ways an extension of the manager-coach trap. When the work pressure starts to build, when we're busy or stressed, investing the time in coaching your people can be one of the first things to fall by the wayside. This is understandable but costly for us as leaders, managers and coaches. We now know that a sense of certainty or consistency is something that we need as human beings in order to be in a productive state of mind. If we flip between coaching when things are going well to telling, or at worse doing nothing at all, when things aren't going so well we're removing this sense of certainty. In doing this we not only put our people into an unproductive frame of mind but we also undermine our own credibility as a leader. Your people will not know what to expect from you, the type of leader you are and what you really believe is important. In other words, you will not be seen as a congruent leader who does what they say they will and this is one of the quickest ways to undermine your position.

We explored some of these challenges in chapter two. But why and how else do we let coaching fall off the to-do list?

One reason may be that on a subconscious level many managers still believe that coaching is distinct and different from doing the real work. I passionately believe that it is both an honour and a privilege to lead any team. In accepting the role of a leader, you commit to put your people first, to invest in them and support them. It's not a matter of then doing your work—supporting your team *is* your work.

Exactly the same is true of coaching. In becoming a manager-coach you are making a commitment to invest in and support your people all of the time, not just when you have time.

Let's consider for a moment how a crisis could be a great coaching opportunity. We know that people learn best when challenged and learn the least when in their comfort or panic zones. But why is this?

When people are in their comfort zone their thinking is not challenged which means that they often complete tasks on autopilot. It's the familiar feeling that we have when we have been driving for several years. You're driving along the motorway and you suddenly catch yourself thinking, 'Where did the last ten miles go?'

When people are forced into the panic zone our old friend, the fight or flight response, kicks in once again. It shuts down and diverts resources from many parts of the brain, inhibiting learning, blocking insights and creative thinking.

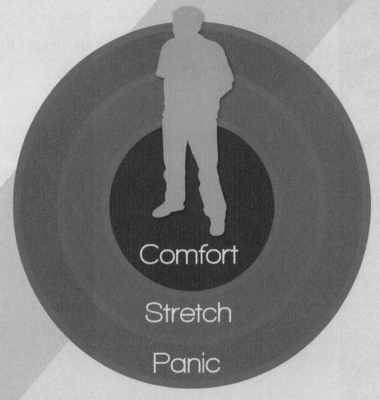

Comfort

Stretch

Panic

Now, I'm not necessarily suggesting that when you are in the middle of a major crisis you stop and spend an hour coaching one of your brightest stars through what they think is the right thing to do next. This doesn't however mean that there is no developmental value to be had from this situation. Once the situation is under control, a post-event coaching session can be an extremely valuable means of developing people in your team.

Consider now a similar situation that is a little lower down the crisis spectrum and how this could also be a fantastic coaching opportunity. A situation that comes with an acceptable amount of pressure could be a brilliant opportunity to develop a team member provided that we give them the right amount of support. So, knowing what we now know about how people learn, why not use the opportunity to coach one of your team members?

Some things to try:

Think about the development needs of your team members and the projects that your team needs to complete. Can you align the two?

Think of a team member who is currently in their comfort zone and give them a project that might stretch them.

Would giving them this project help you as the manager whilst giving them the opportunity to develop?

Would giving them this project help the team achieve its goals?

Chapter Six

Get Clear on the Goals

"**Reach high,**
for stars lie hidden in you.
Dream deep,
for every dream precedes the goal."

Rabindranath Tagore

Whilst getting clear on the goals may seem like an obvious starting point, it can often be overlooked. The biggest shift in my own coaching journey came when I realised just how important and critical this really is. As a time-strapped manager or coach it's all too easy for us to pay just fleeting attention to this before we start jumping into problem solving or solutions mode. This isn't necessarily a bad thing so long as we have properly identified and understood the goals.

Let's look at an example. At some stage in our coaching career most of us will have experienced a session that goes something like this.

You're fifteen minutes into the coaching session and your team member seems to be jumping from one topic to the next. Your head starts spinning and the chatter in your head is going into overdrive.

50

You hear voices in your head saying things like, 'I don't know what to say next... I'm not sure I can help... Oh no, I didn't hear what he just said because I was thinking about what to say myself... I'm really not sure what he needs right now.'

I certainly recall a session like this when I first started coaching. In fact, I remember a number of sessions like this.

The way to overcome this situation is to get really clear on the goals for the session at the beginning of the meeting. If you're working with an individual for a period of time then it's worth investing time in understanding their overall goals for the coaching relationship. Be prepared for the fact that it might take up an entire hour-long session to really identify and then breakdown the goals.

I once asked a client what their goal for our coaching relationship was and they told me, "I want to be a better leader." That was it. They didn't tell me anything else at all. If we had just merrily skipped onto the reality phase of the GROW model, or any other model for that matter, I have no doubt that we both would have become lost in a rambling coaching conversation. Instead of diving straight in we spent a great deal of time exploring in what ways she wanted to be a better leader, in what situations, with what types of people? What was working well for her, what wasn't working so well? What data, evidence or feedback did she have that told her she needed to improve?

Identifying and understanding the real goal can often require more of you as the coach than simply asking what they want to achieve. You may need to ask a series of great coaching questions in order to really understand their goals. You may also need to set realistic expectations of what can be achieved in the time that you have. Getting crystal clear on the outcomes means that you can always steer the session back to the goal and keep things on track as required. This is even more important during the very first session and for the manager-coach. In having this important conversation about their goals for the coaching relationship you may get some unexpected insights from someone who you assumed didn't really need coaching.

Having a clear, well-defined outcome for the coaching session or relationship is like using the North Star to aid navigation. Just as sailors once used it to keep them on track you can use the goals to help whenever you feel lost or unsure where to go next. By simply pausing the conversation and asking permission to focus back on the goals for the session you can regain control. Doing this gives you both time to gather your thoughts and reset the session. If you do find yourself in this situation it is also important to be conscious that you may have identified other goals that your team member would like to work on. If this is the case, it's important to recognise this and check in with your team member and validate your thinking. You may want to share your observations about uncovering some other challenges and explore which is the most important for them to work on.

Some things to try:

Consider identifying the goals as a mini coaching session in its own right.

However much time you have spent in the past identifying the goals with your team member, double it next time and see what impact it has.

When you think you are clear on the goal, pause, think and then ask some more great, clarifying questions.

Some questions to ask:

What do you really want to do?

What would success look / sound / feel like?

When do you want / need to achieve it by?

What do you really want from a career / job?

Why is this important to you?

What would be ten times better than that?

What do you want from this session?

We have *x* minutes today, what would be the most useful things for you to achieve?

If a miracle happened overnight and the challenge went away, how would you know? What would be different?

It seems like we've uncovered a number of challenges today. Which is the most important one for us to focus on?

If you were to prioritise these challenges, what would that order look like?

Chapter Seven

Focus on Performance

> **❝** Don't lower your **expectations** to meet your **performance.**
> **Raise** your **level** of performance to **meet** your expectations.
> **Expect** the **best** of **yourself,** and then do what is **necessary** to make it a **reality. ❞**
>
> *Ralph Marston*

Performance is perhaps one of the **most** misunderstood terms in business today. I would also **suggest** that it is **unlikely** that you will find one common definition of **performance** within any one organisation. Try this experiment. Ask any ten **managers** or **leaders** in your organisation for their **definition of performance** and see how many different responses you get. I'm guessing it will be **ten**, perhaps nine at best.

If your organisation is similar to the **majority**, I suspect that many of your performance definitions will actually be **describing results** or **outcomes.** For example, if you ask a **sales team leader** about their team's performance you'll likely hear things such as, "We've sold fifty percent of this week's target so far and it's only Tuesday," or "We're twenty percent off our target for the week". This isn't describing performance. This is describing the results or the outputs. The danger with this misunderstanding of performance is that we begin to obsess over the outputs and they become our sole focus. In doing so, we miss the opportunity to get really clear on the components or ingredients that enable performance. Yes, your team member may have delivered the goal but if you don't focus on performance you'll miss the fact that they could have done it faster, better, easier, more cheaply, more collaboratively, etc.

So, here's an alternative definition for you to consider.

> "Performance is about doing the things that need to be done in order to achieve the results you desire."

Performance is therefore about getting really clear on the activity that needs to take place in order to enable you to achieve the results you want. But it goes further than that. Performance is about seeking out improvements and making everything you do better so that you are generating the conditions for success. At its best, performance is about identifying what's working well so that you can replicate it over and over again.

Notice that the focus here is on what's going well and on solutions. Far too many personal development plans and annual performance reviews focus on what we need to rectify or be better at. In other words, they are problem focused. The challenge with this is that we leave these performance reviews being an expert in our own failings. We are acutely aware of everything that we are not doing well and everything that is not working for us. And here's the key thing—the results we see in life are a result of where we put our focus. It was Henry Ford who once said,

> "Whether you think you can or think you can't, you are probably right."

So what impact is this likely to have on us?

Consider achieving peak performance as trying to complete a puzzle whose pieces have been hidden around your house. In order to complete the puzzle you must first find all of the pieces. In this respect your role as a manager-coach is to help your team members identify all of the things that work well for them. In doing so, they can approach their challenges from a position of strength and positivity as opposed to a position of weakness. Once you have done this, you can then focus on developing each strength and making each part better and better until you reach the point where success is almost guaranteed.

Some things to try:

Get really clear on the goal and then identify the performance factors that must be present to achieve the outcomes.

When discussing objectives and personal development plans try asking your team member how they can use their strengths to achieve their goals.

Some questions to ask:

What's working well for you right now?

What has worked for you in the past in similar situations?

How could you do more of that?

How can you ensure that you do that more consistently?

What else can you do that will have a positive impact upon your results?

How will you know if it is working or not? What feedback or signs will you see?

When reviewing successful outcomes consider asking, "What could you have done differently to achieve the same outcomes more quickly or easily?"

Chapter Eight

Challenge

"Happiness

is not the absence of problems;
it's the ability to deal with them."

Steve Maraboli

Many managers new to coaching unwittingly make the mistake of thinking it's about teaching people how to do it.

In our busy, time-poor working environment it can be all too easy for managers to approach a coaching session by asking their team member what they think and then suggesting how they would have tackled the problem themselves. In doing so, they then conclude that they have successfully coached their team member. But this isn't coaching. The reality of this approach is that team members leave meetings such as this demotivated, frustrated and thinking, 'Why did they bother asking what I thought if they were just going to tell me how to do it anyway?'

Whilst this approach may enable your team member to quickly complete the task at hand, it is a short-term approach. The other danger of this approach is that your team members begin to rely upon you for the answers to all of their challenges. You may have heard managers saying things like, "Why can't my team members think for themselves? Why do they always come to me for the answers?" You may even have uttered those words yourself.

The reality of this situation is often not that team members can't think for themselves; it is that you have taught them not to think for themselves. Why? Because as busy, time-strapped managers we tell our team members what to do or how we tackled similar challenges in the past. In this respect you are conditioning your team members to respond in the same way as Pavlov did with his dogs. It is like Pavlov asking, "Why do they come running every time they hear a bell?"

If this is your default management style then it is also likely to result in your team approaching their work with fairly low levels of engagement. As a result they may feel unfulfilled at work as a result of having little scope to solve problems and think creatively. To deny a person the opportunity to solve their own problem fundamentally misses what it is to be human. Our ability to solve problems and think creatively is what separates us from every other species on the planet.

The alternative approach is to coach your team members. This is about building another person's own ability to act and enabling them to identify their own solutions. Yes, sometimes a person may need a new technical skill, which is something that we can teach or show them. Whilst this is an extremely valuable way of developing our people, it isn't coaching either.

More often than not, a person needs help thinking through and solving a work challenge on their own, or identifying the thoughts or behaviours that are limiting their performance. This kind of help requires you to ask carefully considered questions, not to tell them what to do.

Here's a key insight. As a coach, manager or leader it's not your job to provide all of the answers. In fact, the sooner that you realise and accept this, the sooner you'll become a great coach, manager and leader.

> "It's not your job to work hard in providing the answers. It's your job to work hard in challenging the person being coached so that they can find their own answers."

The real learning happens when you help the team member to surface their own answers and this is when lasting changes are created. What's more, this is how you can really start to unlock the full potential in every one of your team and achieve great things.

Some questions to ask:

What options do you have?
What else could you do?
What would the world's leading expert in *x* do?
What are the pros and cons of each option?
Would you like another suggestion?

Chapter Nine

Coaching is for Everyone

"Leadership is unlocking people's potential to become better."

Bill Bradley

I t is a common **misconception** amongst many managers who are new to coaching that it's just for those who are **underperforming** in some way. Let me be **clear**, this is **absolutely** not the case. In adopting this mindset, we are immediately **denying** many in our teams of the **opportunity to excel**, to grow and to perform at the level they are **capable** of **reaching**.

If we look at the **history of coaching** we find that it has its roots in **elite sports performance**. How many sports coaches do you see or know of who work with athletes who are **consistently** underperforming? The answer is none or very few. **Professional** sports coaches work with hugely talented individuals and **focus** on moving their performance from **good** to **great** or from great to **world class**.

If this is the case—why would we confine our **coaching skills** to just our **underperformers**?

Everybody in our teams and organisations, **irrespective** of their **current** performance level, is on a **development journey**. Regardless of where they are on this journey they have the potential to make significant performance improvements with the right coaching and support.

Your highest-potential team members and your top performers will have their own challenges and development needs. Think about the challenges that these team members might be struggling to overcome: career growth, a desire to broaden their impact in the organisation, a frustrating working relationship, moving from being a team member to a manager, and many more.

Their challenges are equally as important and equally challenging for them. Helping them to find their own solutions can have as significant an impact on the organisation as raising the performance of those with performance challenges.

In my work developing and leading teams I've learned just how big an impact one person's engagement levels can have on the entire team. Moods, energy levels and states are incredibly contagious and will spread through teams at an alarming rate given the chance. In this respect a frustrated high-potential can be just as damaging to your team as a demotivated underperformer.

There is another huge benefit to coaching your high-potentials. As a group within the organisation these individuals can often be those who have the greatest likelihood of going to work for your competitors. Why? Because they tend to be hugely ambitious, with a desire to progress upwards through the company. The challenge with this is that there are fewer positions for you to promote them into. Without careful management and support, your most talented people can become frustrated and begin seeking opportunities elsewhere.

When trying to tackle high staff turnover McDonald's famously posed a different and slightly unusual question. They asked themselves, "What would we need to do to make our people want to leave the organisation?" From this question they discussed and created a world-class learning and development plan that they then implemented. What happened? Staff turnover plummeted. Their people felt so supported, valued and invested in that they no longer wanted to leave—they wanted to continue working for a great company.

So, if you invest the time in coaching all of your team, you will be rewarded with greater engagement, loyalty, a hunger for improvement and much faster development.

Some things to try:

Set aside one hour to coach all of your team, individually, every two weeks. This should be solely about their own goals and their agenda. It's not a session to discuss your needs or daily business tasks.

Think about the possible challenges that all of your team may be facing or wrestling with.

Think about the challenges you faced when you were in your team members' shoes.

TheCoachingIsForEveryoneStory

Organization: **Major UK Bank**
Coach: **Senior Manager**
Team Member: **Manager**

Alice was a senior manager within a major bank's headquarters who needed to recruit for a new senior team member. Following a number of changes to her team's structure and responsibilities her instinct was to look externally for the new team member rather than promoting from within. Alice was working with a coach herself at the time and during one session she described her goal as this:

> I'm recruiting for a new senior team member and have decided that I am going to go with an external candidate. I would like to talk about how I can keep the two internal candidates motivated when they find out that they are not getting the role.

As the coach explored the goal and the reality of the current situation with Alice, several interesting things came to light. Firstly, she had interviewed the external candidates but she had not yet interviewed the two internal candidates. Secondly, she had not listed the pros and cons of recruiting internally versus externally.

The outcomes of that coaching session shifted Alice's thinking entirely. The key insight for her was the realisation that coaching was not just for her underperformers. It was also for her top performers and those in new roles.

Having carefully considered the benefits and concerns of both options (and deferring her decision until she had completed all of the interviews) she realised a number of things. The internal candidates had ninety percent of the skills and experience needed in the new role but her major concern was the time it would take them to get up to speed in the new role. Interestingly, she also realised that the external candidates had the required technical expertise but lacked the knowledge of the bank, its culture and ways of working. What this meant for Alice was that she would have to devote the same amount of time to supporting the external candidate, possibly even more time, than she would developing the internal candidate. At the same time as supporting them, she would have to work hard at maintaining the motivation of the two disappointed internal candidates—her original goal.

Alice's breakthrough came from the realisation that coaching is a powerful tool for everyone and not just her top performers. She also came to understand that spending time coaching her team members really was an investment and not a cost.

Chapter Ten

Reaching
Elite Performance

"When you're through learning, you're through."

Will Rogers

There are a number of things that separate the elite performers from the average performers. I think that one of the most significant factors is the hunger for learning, development and insights that elite performers have.

When the majority of us are learning a new skill, our hunger for learning gradually decreases with the passage of time. Learning to cook is a great example. In the beginning as we learn to cook we start with the basics. We don't try and be too adventurous and we perhaps don't know what is possible, we don't know what we don't know. As our skills grow we may take it up as a more serious hobby. Our hunger to learn grows, we may start to watch cookery programmes, read books and magazines, go on courses and experiment. Then, as time passes and we find that we can make a pretty good go of making most things from our favourite cookery books, our appetite for learning begins to taper off.

This is the point at which the distinction is drawn between the elite performers and the average performers, as shown in the graph on the next page.

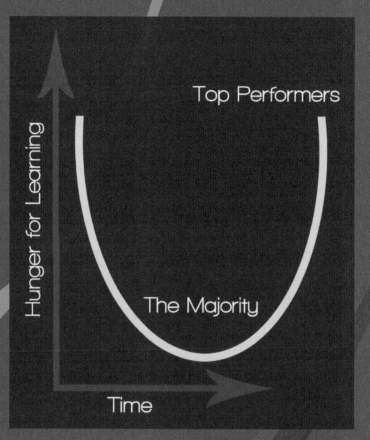

Sticking with the cooking analogy let's think about some of the world's greatest chefs. The likes of Heston Blumenthal and Michael Roux Junior immediately spring to mind. There is something very special and distinct that has enabled them to reach and maintain their level of mastery. It is the fact that their hunger for knowledge, insight and development remains as high with the passage of time as when they first set eyes on a pan.

As a result they continue to seek opportunities for growth, learning and perhaps more importantly, feedback. The most dangerous point in any individual's development is when they think they have nothing left to learn.

For the manager-coach this is a **very real** and common situation. When managers pay too little attention to this **aspect** of their **role** it results in frustrated team members and **increased** staff turnover. This isn't always an **easy** challenge to overcome either as there are only so many positions to **promote** people into and only so many other roles you can move or second your team to. **Ultimately,** when you have a team member whose **hunger for learning** or **development** has **plateaued** you need to find a way to re-energise or excite them.

You can therefore see why it is **important** to focus as much time and effort on coaching your **high-potentials** as those with performance challenges.

Perhaps your next **coaching** session with your high-potentials may **focus** around helping them to **identify** where the next one percent **improvement** may come from and how they will know it's **made a difference.**

Some **questions** to ask:

What is the world's leading expert in your field doing right now?

What else could you do to take your performance from good to great?

If you were to observe yourself for a full day, what performance insights or feedback would you share with yourself?

In a year's time, when you are on stage receiving the award for (insert award), what will you attribute your success to?

What would someone who knows nothing about what you do suggest as a way of improving your performance?

What else would you like to do?

What other projects would you like to use your strengths to tackle?

Chapter Eleven

Be Specific

"Feedback is the breakfast of champions."

Ken Blanchard

One of the biggest mistakes that managers often make when giving feedback or conducting appraisals with their team members is not being specific enough. Not only does vague feedback deny the individual of the information they need to improve their performance, it also activates a strong status and certainty threat. By providing vague, unspecific feedback you immediately trigger your team member's mind-talk. This begins a spiral of events where key parts of the brain are turned off, limiting creative thinking and fresh insights.

The ability to share detailed feedback in a productive, non-threatening manner is critically important for manager-coaches. But why does it sometimes feel so challenging to provide detailed feedback?

Whilst coaching, I have found that there is generally one of two things at the heart of this challenge.

It may be that the manager-coach is genuinely unable to precisely identify the challenge or performance gap that needs to be addressed. If this is the case then the good news for the manager-coach is you don't need to identify the gap because you can coach it out of them! This is a great point at which to just pause and reflect upon the fact that as leaders and coaches we do not need to have all of the answers.

The other reason that we find giving feedback difficult may be as a result of the head tapes that we are running and concerns about how the feedback will be received. If you are struggling to provide your team with specific feedback because of the head tapes that you're running then now may be a great time to revisit chapter four and to think about how you can create more useful and positive tapes.

Whatever the root cause, the outcome tends to be the same. The way that many manager-coaches tackle this challenge is either by being very vague with the feedback that they provide or by avoiding giving the feedback altogether.

So what they actually do is say things like this: "You need to be more of a team player," or "You need to think more about the bigger picture."

Feedback to a team member can be tremendously valuable, especially in helping to raise the team-member's awareness of a potential blind spot. But useful feedback requires accurate descriptions of observed behaviours and the effects.

As a manager-coach, it's important to discipline yourself to look for those specific, observable behaviours before you provide your feedback. The key here really is the observable and specific data. One of the key skills of a great coach is to remain impartial, not making judgments about your team member, their situation or actions. For the manager-coach this can be a real challenge as the impact of your team member's actions will often have an impact on you, the rest of your team and the things that you are accountable for. There is no easy answer to this challenge. It requires self-discipline, and a genuine belief in the benefits of coaching for you to invest your time in the coaching conversations.

Some things to try:

Frame your feedback by saying, "Can I share some observations with you?" or "Would you like me to share some observations?"

If you are not able to provide feedback immediately, make a note of specifically what it was you observed. Then find the earliest opportunity to share the feedback.

Who else could give feedback on your performance?

Where else could you get performance feedback from?

Try using WWW.EBI. What Worked Well was... it could have been Even Better If...

Chapter Twelve

It Goes Both Ways

> **"It is literally true that you can succeed best and quickest by helping others to succeed."**
>
> *Napoleon Hill*

A common mistake new manager-coaches often make is to treat coaching as a one-way exchange.

In the early days of coaching there can be a lot of new information to make sense of and many tools to try and use in your initial coaching sessions. Or at least it can feel that way.

It's no surprise therefore that many manager-coaches start out assuming that the learning, and feedback, in a coaching relationship flows in one direction—from you to your team member.

This misunderstanding denies you the opportunity to develop and grow. In the process of your coaching relationship, you have the chance to profoundly grow and develop. If you fully commit to coaching then you will be transforming yourself from a command and control manager into a supportive leader, enabling and inspiring others to act.

In doing so, you'll find fulfillment through facilitating the growth of those around you in service of a collective goal. You won't just be focusing on what your people achieve; you'll be focusing on how they achieve it. You'll be focusing on performance, which is what great leaders do.

One of the most effective ways of developing your skills as a coach is to work with a coach yourself. Those working as professional coaches often refer to this person as a coaching supervisor. Unfortunately, the term coaching supervisor often seems to have some negative connotations attached to it. The reason I'm sharing this with you now is that I do not want you to believe or accept these negative connotations. I have met many coaches who feel that they can't possibly work with or admit to working with a coaching supervisor. The fear is that in admitting they have a coaching supervisor it suggests that they are not an expert; that they are not perfect.

I have a coaching supervisor. I'm not an expert and I'm not perfect. I do however focus on my performance and I am serious about continuing to develop so I can be the best coach I can possibly be.

For me, it feels somewhat incongruent to *not* work with a coaching supervisor. How can we ask our team members to focus on and reflect upon their performance if we do not do this ourselves? This isn't a sign of weakness; it is a sign of great strength that gives so many positive messages.

As a coach it says, "I believe in coaching. I'm serious about performance and I want to keep developing so that I can support you."

As a leader it says, "I'm authentic. I'm comfortable in sharing my development needs. I don't necessarily have all the answers and I'm cool with that."

I began my career in the British Army at the age of sixteen. At fifteen I met with a major from an army recruiting team whose job was to prepare me for a two-day assessment centre. Something he said has stayed with me throughout my entire career, both in and out of the Army. It has also helped me in my journey as a coach. This is what he said.

"Ben, remember that as a leader you do not need to have all of the answers."

I think that this is absolutely true of a leader and manager but it's even more significant for a coach. For coaches I believe it should read as follows:

"Remember that, as a coach, you absolutely do not need to have all of the answers."

In summary, I believe that as coaches we must be open to learning and feedback ourselves. By actively seeking feedback from our team members it sets a precedent and creates a feedback culture. In doing this we create an environment where feedback is the norm and it makes providing feedback so much easier.

As manager-coaches we should regularly reflect on our performance, seek feedback and work with a coaching supervisor. This could well be another manager-coach, a friend or an external coach. It's likely that you will have a network of peers and colleagues who are all having similar coaching conversations. What a great source of knowledge, support and learning this network could be.

Ultimately, who your coaching supervisor is does not matter all that much, it is having somebody to talk to about your coaching performance that really matters.

Some things to try:

Find a colleague with whom you can discuss your coaching performance at least four times a year.

Make time to reflect upon your coaching sessions and write down your reflections.

Ask your team members for feedback.

Ask your team member if you can record your coaching session so that you can review it later.

Some questions to ask:

Could I have done anything better to support you?

What could I have done to make this session even more valuable for you?

Do you have any feedback for me as a coach that you would like to share?

If you were in my shoes, what would you have asked that would have been really valuable?

Chapter Thirteen

Be of Service

"Serve to Lead"

Motto of the
Royal Military Academy Sandhurst

One of the most significant and costly mistakes you can make as a manager-coach is neglecting to ask the person being coached how you can be most helpful to them. This is one of the most powerful, yet most overlooked, questions that a manager-coach can ask their team members. For example, when did you last ask this question?

"What can I do to really help you right now?"

One of the best coaches, trainers and facilitators I have had the privilege to work with is highly skilled at uncovering and understanding the outcomes that the person he is coaching is looking for. Here are just a few of his brilliant opening questions:

What would make this session really valuable for you?

What can I do to make today an eleven out of ten? What would be the cherry on top of the cake for you?

What would make this coaching session outstandingly valuable for you?

You need to **be aware** that as a manager-coach you have a particular challenge and face a **potential** pitfall that does not exist for external coaches. That is the challenge of failing to be of **total service** to your team member or of hijacking their **agenda.** As a manager-coach you absolutely must **approach** your sessions with a great deal of clarity and **integrity.** It is not uncommon for manager-coaches to find that their interests and those of their team members are in **conflict.** For example, your team member may be trying to **clarify and understand** their long-term career goals, whilst at the same you may **clearly** see them as a **successor** for your position.

As a manager and a coach, you need to **remain** aware of this potential for conflict and the danger of **steering** the outcomes in a direction that meets your needs. This means that you **need to provide clarity** about which hat you are wearing at any particular time. Your **role** as a managerial coach is not to impose your **will** on your team member in the **guise of coaching.** To do so would be to **undermine** your position as a **leader** and devalue the coaching approach that you have **adopted.**

Providing Feedback

Whilst your job as a coach is **absolutely** to support your people, it is also your job to provide them with **performance** insights and feedback that they cannot see for themselves or that others are perhaps not prepared to give. This can be a real challenge in the **early stages** of our coaching journey because giving **feedback** is something that many managers feel a little uncomfortable **doing.**

87

We generally tend to feel less confident undertaking new activities or when in new situations because they feel unfamiliar to us. By committing to giving more feedback, the very thing that makes us feel uncomfortable, we are able to expand our comfort zone. It will not instantly make giving feedback the most comfortable thing in the world (although it may for some), but over time, by consistently doing it we are able to expand our comfort zone.

There is one other amazing benefit in adopting a coaching management style. Your team members start to expect, want and ask for feedback from you. In coaching your team members and offering feedback you not only expand your comfort zone, you expand theirs too. This creates a virtuous circle where giving feedback leads your team to seek out feedback making the process easier and easier for all involved. Feedback ceases to be something that they receive twice a year as part of the appraisal process and becomes just the way you do things.

Having invested the time and effort in developing your coaching skills, it's not surprising that your focus can, at times, be on how you are doing as a coach. In the early days of my coaching journey I would often find myself listening to my own mind-talk during a session. I'd be listening to a voice in my head saying things like 'What model should I try and use next? What question should I ask next? How am I doing right now?' or 'Am I any good at coaching?'

But here's the thing that I eventually realised. That's the exact opposite of what I should actually have been doing.

The very best coaches, the truly world-class coaches, put all of their energy into helping the person being coached to become great. They focus fully on their team member and put all of their effort into listening to what they are saying—which creates a virtuous circle. By listening and watching intently, they hear and see exactly what is being said. This in turn means that they do not need to worry about what questions to ask as the questions become obvious, they just seem to appear in their minds.

In focusing more on our team members and less on ourselves we are being of genuine service to them. In doing so we will become great coaches. The time to reflect upon our own performance is after the coaching session, not during it.

Some things to try:

Be of service by giving full control of planning the agenda for one-to-one meetings to your team members.

Before giving some feedback ask your team member, "Can I share an observation with you?"

Look for opportunities to give more feedback—it will strengthen your feedback muscle.

Create a safe, regular forum in team meetings where your team can provide each other, and you, with feedback.

TheConflictingPrioritiesStory

Organization: **Major Travel Company**
Coach: **Sales Director**
Team Member: **Sales Team Leader**

John, a sales director in a travel company, was about to leave his organisation after many years service. As a consequence of his departure, a joint venture project with another company in the group would be unlikely to continue unless a very talented member of his team, Sarah, moved to the other company.

Several months prior to John's departure, Sarah came to him asking for advice about whether she should take the role in the other company or not. John said that at the start of his management journey he would have immediately given advice and suggestions of what to do, based upon the fact that it was advice that Sarah was asking for.

However, in this case, John moved into coaching mode and began asking a number of great questions.

Why is this a difficult question for you? What are your concerns? What are the things that you're thinking about?

John's main aim was to help Sarah arrive at her own solution that she felt confident about committing to.

During the course of the coaching conversation it became clear to Sarah (and John) that the move to the other organisation would not be the right thing for her. The consequence of this realisation was that Sarah would ultimately leave her current company as her job would cease to exist.

It was at this point that John became conscious of his conflicting priorities as a manager-coach. On the one hand he believed in supporting and looking after his team so supporting Sarah's decision felt right. On the other hand, despite leaving the organisation he had a great deal of loyalty to the company and Sarah's departure would have an impact upon them.

John's final decision was ultimately born out of his beliefs and values:

> By that point I'd got to the position where I was very much in the belief that if you know there is somebody who is no longer motivated by the job they are doing, there is no point in trying to talk them into staying in that role. You're better off helping them to go where they need to be and finding someone else for that role.

Chapter Fourteen

Be Proactive, Be Flexible

> **"Be infinitely flexible and constantly amazed."**
>
> *Jason Kravitz*

As a manager-coach you have the unique opportunity to be proactive and not rely solely on your team member to identify their needs and initiate the coaching conversations.

We have already discussed a number of times that it is important to be responsive to your team member's needs and not to drive the agenda yourself, but that doesn't mean that you can't be proactive when the opportunity arises.

You can watch your team member in their working environment which is an advantage you have over external coaches. This allows you to observe their performance and provide focused, developmental feedback. So, if you are conscious of this, on the occasions when they arrive at your one-to-ones with nothing to discuss you can suggest topics based upon what you know of them and their performance.

At this point it is worth reflecting once again on the most common route to management that we explored in chapter two. That is the journey from being a doer or functional expert, to a team leader, then manager, senior manager, director and beyond. This journey means that it's highly likely that you will have experienced very similar, if not the same, challenges to those your team are facing. It's also highly likely that you may know some of the challenges that they will face before they do. Your team member may not know when they are facing a particular challenge, heading for a landmine, or about to make a big mistake—but you probably will. So, it's important that you remain proactive and ready to spot trouble on the horizon.

This unique position that you can find yourself in as a manager-coach presents the danger of you driving the agenda. However, it also presents a fantastic opportunity for you to serve those that you lead. For the expert manager-coach this is about moving seamlessly between coaching and mentoring. It is about flexing your style and utilising the skills as both a coach and mentor. But what are the differences between coaching and mentoring?

Coaching is characterised by a partnership approach whereby the coach asks questions of the coachee and, in doing so, challenges their thinking to enable them to arrive at their own solutions. In this respect, a coach doesn't necessarily need to have experience of the coachee's work, environment or specific challenges.

In contrast, a mentor will share their specific experiences of tackling challenges that are similar to, or perhaps the same as, those facing the mentee. A mentor will share their experience, advice and learning of similar situations in order to help the mentee develop. Another notable distinction between the two is that coaches focus on providing support and encouragement whereas a mentor will focus on providing specific advice. So what does this mean in practice?

On the occasions when your team member comes to a meeting with nothing to talk about, or at least nothing that they have prepared in advance, you are in a great position to support them. The key coaching skill of being able to use enquiry to surface what's going on for them at that moment, whilst drawing on your own experience to identify unrecognised challenges, is incredibly powerful.

In these situations it really is the blend of coaching and mentoring coupled with a collaborative mindset that creates the conditions for success. As a manager-coach it's important to resist the temptation to switch into *tell* mode and assume that the way *you* tackled a situation, is the best way or the only way. By highlighting the challenges, sharing some of your experiences, and continuing to coach you can achieve some amazing results. This approach can often lead to some truly innovative ideas and breakthrough solutions for them, for your team and for your business.

In summary, being proactive can appear, on the surface at least, to be the opposite of being of service. But in reality, it is not that clear cut. Whilst it is extremely valuable to prepare for any coaching session, and I would always encourage you to do this no matter how experienced you are, it is also vitally important that you remain flexible.

Entering the session with a view on the kind of conversation that you want or could have does not mean that you are failing to be of service or hijacking the agenda. But once you get in the room, your main job is to really listen to and understand your team member. Your job is to help them tackle the challenges that they are facing whilst still being ready to point out the unknown. In doing this, you really will be of service to them. In doing this you really will be a leader.

Some things to try:

Set aside time before coaching sessions to think back to when you were doing a job similiar to your team member and ask yourself these questions:

What were the mistakes I made that I could have avoided?
What do I wish I knew then?
What were the challenges that I didn't see coming?
What did I muddle through that could have been better?
What would I like to have had another shot at with the power of hindsight?
What do I know about the organisation or sector (that they don't), that will be of value to them?

Ask yourself what experience, insight, observation or piece of feedback you have that would be valuable to share?

Consider what you need to do, if anything, to stay in coaching mode and out of tell mode.

TheBeProactiveBeFlexibleStory

Organization: **UK Retailer**
Coach: **Commercial Director**
Team Member: **Commercial Manager**

David, a commercial director, in a large UK retailer described his approach and philosophy to managing and leading the people within his team like this:

> I think that people are much more willing to work for you, to achieve and be focused on doing a good job, if they feel happy in their surroundings; if they feel happy where they are at that moment in life. Someone who spends their time constantly thinking about whether or not they are doing a good job, where their next career move is, and whether or not the current role is the right one for them is not going to be focused on delivering in the role. I think that if they feel that they are being developed and have an idea of where they are going they are much more likely to perform. Having an idea about where they are going is not just about moving on or being promoted. That is not everybody's aspiration and for those people it is about affirming that they are still developing and doing a great job. I think that my job as a leader is to create an environment where this can happen and carve out the time to support my people. If you lose touch of that then you can lose touch with them, what's important for them, and what they are doing.

From the very beginning of my interview with David it became apparent to me that he has a very proactive approach to leading and developing his team. On several occasions he used phrases like "carve out time" and "creating an environment where they can develop." The next question that I asked David was how did he go about doing this?

> I make sure that I spend at least one hour per week with each of the people that I have reporting to me. We don't always use all of the time, it depends very much on the individual, but I ensure that I create the space regardless. I don't intend for that time to be used to discuss their objectives, the tasks in hand or what's going on in work. It can be about that, but it doesn't have to be—I certainly do not put any restrictions on the agenda. If they want to talk about personal development, career plans or even how they are feeling in that moment—all of those are fine with me. I like to be led by what they want to do.

David went on to share a fantastic example of how he proactively prepares for these one-to-one meetings whilst balancing a coaching and mentoring style. He described a time when he had somebody working for him, Sarah, who just wasn't happy working in the culture and environment of the organisation. It wasn't a case that she wasn't good at her job, because she was. Equally it wasn't about those around Sarah giving her a hard time, because they weren't. It was more the case that she couldn't understand how others were working in the organisation, and they couldn't understand her. Because of Sarah's personality it came out almost as a moan when she was describing her situation. This is how David described the situation, what he did and the outcome his actions created.

> It almost got to the stage where every week I would sit and listen to Sarah moan. But I did sit and listen every week because I felt it was the right thing to do and it enabled her to get it off of her chest. I waited every week until she had finished and then stopped. I then said let's take a step back. The first thing I did was to make it really clear that I had listened to what she said and that I understood how Sarah was feeling so she felt supported. I absolutely think that is part of my role— to be there and support my people. The second thing I would do is to reflect back what I had heard, along with my understanding of what

she had said. Then, the third thing I did was to share what I would have done in her situation or how I would have tackled the same challenge. I was trying to recommend a way that she could get around the problems she was having with certain people and the organisation's culture.

But I knew from fairly early on that I could sit there and do that every week but Sarah just really wasn't comfortable in the culture of our organisation. It just wasn't her, and what we were talking about every week were the symptoms of that. So, as time went on I started to prepare more in advance for our meetings and began adding a fourth element to the discussion. I would say that we had tried everything I knew and yet we were still having challenges. So, I asked her to really think about what it was that she wanted. For me, it felt like Sarah wasn't happy in the role and I wanted to share my observations with her and for her to understand that I recognised that. We discussed the fact that I wanted to do something to support her, but, within the framework that I had, I wasn't sure if I could offer her the solution she wanted or needed.

At the end of the day, we came out of that situation. There was no breakdown in the relationship, she was happy and able to continue working for me and we got the best out of the situation. The real outcome was that as a result of our sessions she came to the point in her own mind where she said, 'OK—I've had enough,' and she went and got a great job elsewhere, outside of the organisation. The great thing for me is that we have stayed friends after that, in fact we went to a festival together with some of her ex-colleagues too and we all had a great time. So I was pleased in that respect that we maintained a good relationship and got the best out of something that was never going to work.

There are so many great things that we can take away from David's experiences of coaching and mentoring Sarah. The first is his blend of coaching and mentoring. By using the coaching skills of questioning and active listening he was not only able to understand her situation, but, perhaps more importantly, demonstrate to Sarah that he understood her situation. In doing so he showed a great sense of empathy that helped Sarah to feel supported within the team despite her frustrations. Whilst utilising his coaching skills to understand her situation he then gave suggestions based upon his knowledge and experience of the organisation. In doing so, he blended the skills of a coach and a mentor to great effect.

There are other useful lessons hidden in David's story. The skill involved in identifying the goals as well as the confidence not to be afraid of revisiting them. You will recall how his approach changed over time—specifically when he mentioned the fact that they had tried everything he knew, how it still wasn't working, and that he wanted Sarah to really think about what it was that she wanted. This was an example of a great coach reclarifying the goal.

In this fantastic case study we have heard how David focused on his team member, took a proactive approach, refocused Sarah on her goals whilst the whole time was being of service to his team member.

Chapter Fifteen

The GROW Model

> **"A coach is part advisor, part sounding board, part cheerleader, part manager and part strategist."**
>
> *The Business Journal*

The GROW model is perhaps one of the most widely used coaching models within organisations and by coaches in the early part of their coaching career. Its success, I believe, is partly due to its simplicity and versatility. In the early stage of a manager-coach's career I believe that the model provides a simple, yet powerful structure to base your conversations around. GROW stands for:

Goal

Reality
Current

Options (or Obstacles)

Will (or Way Forward)

GROW

Establishing the Goal is about working with your team member to identify the behaviour or situation that you want to change. In doing so, it is important to identify a clear goal. If you have done this well, you should both have a clear idea of how you will be able to tell if the goal has been achieved.

The next step is to explore the Reality by asking your team member to describe their current situation. This is an important step. All too often people try to solve a problem without fully understanding their starting point. Imagine how difficult it would be trying to plan a journey in your car if you did not know where you were starting from? Trying to achieve a goal without understanding the reality, or current situation is exactly the same. It's often the case that the solution, or the keys to the solution, are hidden amongst the current reality.

Once your team members have explored the current reality, or the start point, then it is time to explore the Options for achieving the goal. This is about discussing all of the possible options and asking your team member, "What else?" This helps them identify other possibilities that they may not have considered without your support. Once you have identified all of the options, your task moves on to helping them identify which options are most suitable for them.

The final step in the process is about discussing the Will and helping them to commit to the actions that you have discussed. Having a clear goal and even a plan to achieve it, isn't always enough to make change happen.

105

This **final step** is about helping your team member commit to the **actions** that you have discussed. It may be by **discussing** what you or others can do to help, it may be about **clearing** obstacles or it may be about recognising and **celebrating success** along the way.

I said that discussing the **will** was the final step, but that's not strictly true. Whilst the **model** normally starts with the **goal** and ends with **will**—it doesn't have to be a model that you follow **linearly**. At any stage of the model you may well find yourself moving **backwards** as you seek to **reclarify** or check the **goals**. Similarly, you may find yourselves suddenly fast-forwarding to will because the mere **process** of discussing the goal or reality has mad the obvious **next steps** appear. Whilst the **GROW** model provides a **framework** and set of steps to follow, you should not allow it to drive the coaching conversation. The **model** is a **tool** to enable great **conversations**, not a process to be rigidly adhered to.

Whilst I have given a brief **overview** of the **model**, my aim is not to provide you with a step-by-step guide for coaching with **GROW**. I have however included an **insightful** case study that shares one coach's personal journey of **practice** and **discovery** using the model. As with the other chapters in this book, I hope that this will help to **accelerate** your development as a manager-coach.

TheGROWModelStory

Organization: **Major Telecoms Company**
Coach: **Training Manager**
Team Member: **Customer Service Operator**

This story is a little different to the others in the book in that the author's name has not been changed. The words below are those of my friend and colleague, Richard Nugent, who is one of the very best coaches I know.

What I find so inspiring about his story is his readiness to freely share his early and slightly awkward coaching sessions. It can provide all of us with an injection of confidence. Even the best coaches started somewhere, and that somewhere may be very familiar.

> I started coaching back in my days as a trainer in a large call centre. I was expected to be a great coach and to help staff improve their performance. The trouble was that my experience of coaching had been limited to the sports world—where coaching meant that the coach demonstrated a technique, had the person try it out and then tell them what they did wrong in order to correct it. I was sure that coaching in a business context couldn't be the same, could it?
>
> Around that time, I experienced a two-day coaching skills programme— teaching me the GROW model, some listening skills and, of course, the feedback sandwich. I was released out onto the call centre floor to listen in on calls and provide coaching to those lucky advisors whose customer interactions I had monitored.

I tried to follow GROW as my trainer had taught me, and the session often went something like this:

Coach: What's your goal for this session?

Advisor: Errr... For you to tell me how I have done whilst you've been listening in.

Coach: Hmmmm... OK. How do you think the call went?

Advisor: Fine, I think.

Coach: Good. Good. What are the opportunities for you to improve next time?

Advisor: Look—what the hell are you on about? Just tell me if I did OK or not.

Then I would give them a feedback sandwich...

Well, I thought the opening was really nice—and you closed it well. You gave the customer lots of incorrect information though. However, your voice sounded really professional.

Of course, I wasn't always this bad—and over time I developed my rapport skills and ability to give feedback in a way that added value for the advisors, and ultimately for the customers.

So, there is a place for really great performance feedback, and for coaching on the intricacies of a specific process. It forms the meat and drink for many people in business today and the chances are that your journey as a manager-coach started with the GROW model in a similar way to me. However, this was just the beginning of my coaching journey.

Many years after ditching GROW, I finally saw it applied the way I'm sure it was meant to be. I worked with a coach whose opening question was, 'How can I help?' They moved elegantly through the stages of the model, jumping back and forth as the client required, drawing from a huge bank of high-quality questions.

They created new resources in the clients they worked with, helping them to explore new options before helping them to decide on the most congruent option and then encouraging the client towards absolute commitment to action. Most impressive of all was that the coaching was content-free. They never once advised or led—she simply asked great questions.

Chapter Sixteen

Beyond GROW

"To know oneself is to study oneself in action with another person."

Bruce Lee

Whilst I believe that the GROW model is a fantastic tool for any coach to use at the beginning of their career, I also believe that it's important to master it and move on. But let me be clear. When I say move on, I do not mean abandon the model all together. Here is what I really mean.

As a leader, I have always led and managed my teams with a style akin to coaching. In the early part of my career this was due to the belief I had in those I was privileged enough to lead. It certainly wasn't due to a conscious awareness of what coaching was or its benefits. At that time I believed my team had great ideas and were capable of achieving amazing results with just a little support from me. I also fundamentally believed, and still do, that I did not have a monopoly on great ideas—remember the major from the army recruiting team in chapter twelve?

Many years later, having left the Army and found myself leading an HR function within a large travel company, I became conscious that coaching existed as a development tool. I did some internet-based research and read a dusty copy of *Coaching for Dummies* that one of my team found in the back of a cupboard (I'm not sure if she was subtly trying to tell me something). At this point I rather clumsily started to experiment with and use the GROW model to coach and mentor colleagues in my team and the organisation. Reflecting back on those early attempts using the model the experiences that my team members had were not dissimilar to those described in the GROW model case study. I rigidly moved my team members through the various steps of the model feeling pleased that we had arrived at the will stage with some commitments in place. In doing this I made so many mistakes and lost touch with what had been working well for me in the past. My focus switched from having a conversation and listening to my team member to using a model. It suddenly became less about them and more about moving them through a process—all of which was fundamentally unproductive and missed the point of coaching entirely.

Sometime later I realised that the model wasn't working that well for me, but more importantly, it wasn't working for those whom I was coaching. At this point I decided to abandon the model and go back to what I had intuitively always done.

The Development Coach

As with Richard's story in the last case study, a long time after giving up on GROW, I finally saw it being expertly used. I watched a number of coaches skilfully use the model as a supporting framework. They seamlessly moved backward and forwards through the model in a manner that was designed to do nothing else than help the person they were coaching. Because they were comfortable with the model they were able to focus intently on the individual that they were coaching. This in turn meant that they were able to ask the right questions at the right time that would best help their clients. They helped them identify new solutions and possible approaches that they had not previously considered. Finally, they explored these options in a manner that enabled the individual being coached to commit to those actions which best suited them, and, most significantly, those that they could commit to. This was much more than simply arriving at will and testing their commitment as I had done in the past. But perhaps most impressive of all was that the coaching was content-free. As Richard observed, they never once advised or led—they simply asked great questions.

Some years later, whilst completing a coaching course myself, I finally mastered the GROW model and felt really comfortable using it. When I say mastered it, I actually mean several things. Firstly, I understood the model and had embedded it into my subconscious thinking. Secondly, I understood that it was a framework to support a session and not a strict methodology to be followed linearly to control the session. Thirdly, and perhaps most significantly, I understood that it was one of many coaching tools that I could blend together as the circumstances required. To this day I still find that the most powerful of those other tools is the ability to focus on the person I am coaching, listening intently.

I learned that my new-found coaching persona was often given the label of Development Coach. Great developmental coaches spend more time focused on what their client is saying (or not saying) than to the coaching model itself. They are masters at matching and mirroring, and, perhaps most important of all, they help their clients to focus on what is possible— not just what the problem is.

My colleague, Richard Nugent, once said that in this second phase of evolution the emphasis is on development. When he discovered that coaching didn't just have to be remedial, his fire was well and truly lit. At that point he was certain that he wanted to be a coach. But what he didn't yet appreciate were the possibilities that still lay ahead when he fully developed the new skills he was acquiring.

The Master Coach

The next phase in the life cycle or evolution of a coach is that to Master Coach. If your approach to leadership, developing yourself and your team encompasses several of the points overleaf, then you are probably a Master Coach already.

You know the fastest single way to build deep rapport with your team members.

You have an extensive bank of great coaching questions to draw upon—but more often that not, the most elegant resource-unlocking question just pops into your head intuitively.

You are a master of your own emotional state and are able to strongly influence that of your team members.

You are able to help your team members create outstanding performance breakthroughs even when you are not the expert, or even experienced in, the challenge that they are facing.

You draw on the work of great coaches and Transformational Coaches such as Nancy Kline, Michael Neill, David Clutterbuck, Sir John Whitmore and other valuable sources such as the Solutions Focus and Flow.

You are comfortable moving seamlessly between coaching and mentoring as the situation dictates and as the need arises.

You are able to share detailed feedback and observations with your team members in a highly productive and non-threatening manner.

Whilst your focus as a Master Coach is still firmly on respecting your team member's map of the world—and not suggesting or leading them down any particular route—you can help them to commit more fully. When I first arrived at this point in my coaching journey I naively thought that coaching wasn't about the models, it was just about listening and asking great questions. I went as far as to argue the case for abandoning the models; suggesting that new coaches should just focus on listening to their team members. My belief was that in doing so, the right questions would just appear in your mind. But let me state this next point quite clearly.

I was totally wrong.

To get here takes dedication, practice, study and commitment. I only reached the point at which those great coaching questions appeared because I had spent time using the models, practising and most importantly, reflecting on my own coaching practice. The models are an important, no, vital part of the evolution of a coach. Abandon them completely at your peril.

All that said, if you are at the point of being a Master Manager-Coach, I believe that you are already making the workplace and the world a better place.

TheMasterCoachStory

Organization: **Central Government Department**
Coach: **Civil Servant**
Team Member: **All of his team**

James is a senior manager within one of the major central government functions. Unlike many of those interviewed for the case studies in this book, he has received some formal training as a coach along with an extended period of reflective coaching practice. This is how James described his coaching journey and his approach to leading his department.

I think that I have always had a management style that encompasses coaching, even before I had any formal training as a coach. Having now trained as a coach though, it is now even more obvious to me that this is a far better way of managing the team, the work and achieving the outcomes. A coaching approach to management creates a real sense of buy-in from the team and it also allows me to take a more appropriate view of the work across our portfolio. I do not need to be in the detail of what all of my team are doing—they have the expertise and experience for that. Coaching has allowed me to have more of an overview of the work in our portfolio, ensure that the right links are across the department and to support individuals' development. As a result of applying my coaching skills I'm now finding that my team are resolving many issues themselves. I physically see their faces light up when they realise they have solved their own challenges. There is much more of an acceptance of responsibility, yet at the same time they feel like there is a weight that has been lifted off of their shoulders. I think that this is due to them having the freedom to make their own decisions, balanced by support from me and the confidence that they can solve their own problems.

James has clearly been on a significant journey as a coach and it was interesting to hear him say that it is now obvious that coaching is a much better way to manage. Earlier in this book I described how adopting a coaching style can initially feel like it is more work for you as the leader. I think that James' story is proof of the value that it brings in the medium-to-long term. We heard from James how his team now largely solve their own challenges, how much more engaged they are with a greater sense of buy-in and their willingness to accept responsibility. What manager would not want a team with those skills and attitudes?

James also shared with me a little of his journey beyond GROW and towards becoming a Master Coach. Here's what he said:

> As a result of my coaching training and having logged in excess of 100 hours reflective coaching practice I find that I use the various tools on much more of an unconscious level. I don't consciously think about the models that I am using or even about using them in a structured way. It is only by later reflecting on my coaching sessions that I become aware of the fact that I am blending different tools together, at different times, in order to achieve the outcomes for my team member. Whilst I'm using the tools less consciously in the session, I am now much more conscious of reflecting on my own skills and thinking about how I can improve.
>
> The other significant change, which affects all that I do, is that I am now far more aware of the questions that I ask and how I ask them.
>
> The final thing that I would also say is that I am now far less concerned about whether I am coaching or mentoring. Whilst I am always clear about which hat I'm wearing at any point in time, I'm happy to move between the two and balance the coaching and mentoring. Whether I'm coaching or mentoring is less important to know, so long as I am helping the individual to move forwards and achieve their outcomes.

A Transformational Coach will do whatever is necessary to help their team member or client create what they want. Often this starts by helping them to understand the power of creating. If you are new to this distinction between reporting and creating the closest single phrase I'd use to sum it up is the one credited to Kathlyn Hendricks:

> "Your life is a reflection of what you are already committed to."

Transformational Coaches have a deep understanding of just what is possible. They realise that, when you are swimming in the sea, it's hard to see the water—so often the most transformational work is the most obvious. In this respect they are focusing 100% on the individual, not themselves, their ego or calling themselves a coach. Another distinction is that they work best when their team members are ready to be coached.

This is the point at which leader and coach become one and the same. The two-sided coin that I referred to in the opening chapter of this book has been fully forged. They realise that as a great manager-coach or leader, they exist to be of service to those that they lead. The Transformational Coach uses metaphor, stories and their own life experiences on top of their keenly honed master-coaching skills to help their team members realise their full potential.

To reach this point they have also become totally comfortable with who they are as a leader. They do not hold back in fear that their team members may become more successful than they are. They do not recruit team members who are B players for fear of being upstaged. Their goal is to help all of their team members reach their full potential, for themselves and for the organisation. If this means that their team members achieve more than they do themselves—then they see that as a sign of their own success as a leader.

The final thing they realise is that they can learn just as much from their team members as their team members learn from them; it goes both ways.

The Next Level

I'd like to end with an admission. I don't know with total clarity what the next stage of the development of a coach or manager-coach is. What I do know is that there is another level and I'm just starting to catch glimpses of what that may be. I'm certainly not there yet, but I'm working hard to get there with my own coach. Sharing my thoughts with you in this book is part of my journey and I'm looking forward to finding out where this will take us.

The most important thing about this for me is that I'm comfortable not knowing and I'm comfortable telling you that I don't know. And here's why:

> " Ben, remember that as a leader you do not need to have all of the answers. "
> *The Army Recruiting Major*

Appendix

This section includes a collection of great coaching questions that I have used during my own coaching journey. Hopefully, many of them will be of use early in your coaching career. They will prompt your thinking and enable you to develop your own bank of powerful coaching questions. But perhaps more significantly, I hope that they inspire you to start coaching your people and in doing so, help you to become the leader you are capable of being and becoming.

Goal Questions

What do you really want to do?

What would success look / sound / feel like?

When do you want / need to achieve it by?

What do you really want from a career / job?

Why is this important to you?

What would be ten times better than that?

What do you want from this session?

We have x minutes today, what would be the most useful things for you to achieve?

What would be your ideal outcome?

What is your future perfect scenario?

How will you know if this session has been useful to you?

What would need to happen for you to leave this session feeling that it was outstandingly valuable?

How can I be of most help to you today?

Reality Questions

What's happening now?

What exactly do you mean by ...?

When you say..., what exactly do you mean?

How often do you face this challenge?

What's your current situation?

Who else is involved?

What are the three most important things about the issue?

What have you done so far? How successful has this been?

What results have you achieved so far?

What's helping?

What's getting in the way?

What are the obstacles you find yourself facing?

What's missing in this situation?

What is really going on?

What are you not telling me?

What's holding you back?

Options Questions

What options do you have?

What three things could you do?

What else could you do?

What would the world's leading expert in x do?

What if time, resources, etc.,h were not an issue?

What are the pros and cons of each option?

Would you like another suggestion?

If it didn't matter if you failed, what would you do?

Have you experienced a similar challenge before? If so, what did you do then that worked?

If you took just one tiny action, what would it be?

What's currently working for you that you could do more of?

Is there anything that you could stop doing that would have a positive impact?

Will Questions

What are you going to do next? By when?

Will this get you the outcome you want? If not, what else will?

What barriers or obstacles might you face and how will you overcome these?

Who else needs to know about / support your plans?

What support do you need? (Think about resources, people, etc.)

What could I do to support you?

What commitment on a scale of 1-10 do you have to taking the agreed actions?

What would move you one point further up this scale?

What prevents this being a ten?

What would you need to do to make this a ten?

What could you do to increase your commitment?

To what extent has this session achieved the outcomes we set?

About the Author

Ben Morton is an international team-development consultant and coach whose clients range from small and solo business owners to FTSE 100 companies and international brands.

He is a Chartered Member of the CIPD (Chartered Institute of Personnel and Development) with approaching two decades of experience in leadership, learning and management. His broad range of experience is gained from roles including Group Head of HR and Training for a global subsidiary of TUI Travel and the Global Leadership Training Academy at Tesco.

He began his career in the British Army and trained at the Royal Military Academy Sandhurst. Ben completed two operational tours of Iraq, initially as a Platoon Commander and again as an Operations Officer leading 180 soldiers before resigning his Commission as a Captain in 2006.

As a leader, Ben's style has always been based upon coaching. He believes that those he has had the privilege to lead always had the capability to find their own solutions; they just needed a little support. Ben is clear that the route to unlocking the potential in teams and individuals is based upon giving people time, support and asking the right questions. In addition to his practical coaching experience he is also qualified as a Level 7 Executive Coach and Leadership Mentor through the Institute of Leadership and Management.

At TwentyOne Leadership, Ben specialises in two key areas. Firstly, he works with clients to enable them to understand what is required to develop high performing, highly effective teams. Secondly, he helps individuals moving into their first leadership role or those whose careers have progressed rapidly, finding themselves leading large and often very experienced teams.

Also from mPowr

The Key: To Business and Personal Success
Martyn Pentecost

This unique book challenges the simple mantras and quick-fix strategies that are so often presented in contemporary business and personal development.

The Key gives you an individual profiling method for creating enduring success in all areas of life. Your world, your business, your experience, your life, are complex and ever-changing. Using the powerful resources at your fingertips you can match the depth of your complexity, tailor your unique profile and develop effective strategies that flow from your optimal performance.

Not only is *The Key* very different in attitude and perspective, it also encompasses an innovative approach to business development—using metaphor to prime your brain for the powerful resources and philosophies that propel you towards your goals and desires in truly profound ways. The enchanted tales of *The Key* enable you to layer the multifaceted logic in ways that make your learning experience much easier and more fun!

Whether building a business plan, developing your career, getting fit or attaining amazing relationships, *The Key* offers solutions unlike anything you have previously encountered. Based on more than a decade of research, *The Key* was originated by personal development mentor and author, Martyn Pentecost.

Lightning Source UK Ltd.
Milton Keynes UK
UKOW06f0309130915

258484UK00012B/71/P